4/19

W9-BTL-347

EXPLORING WORLD CULTURES

Argentina

Joanne Mattern

Cavendish
Square

New York

Published in 2019 by Cavendish Square Publishing, LLC
243 5th Avenue, Suite 136, New York, NY 10016

Copyright © 2019 by Cavendish Square Publishing, LLC

First Edition

Library of Congress Cataloging-in-Publication Data

Names: Mattern, Joanne, 1963- author.
Title: Argentina / Joanne Mattern.
Description: First edition. | New York : Cavendish Square, [2019] | Series: Exploring world cultures | Includes bibliographical references and index. | Audience: Grades 2-5.
Identifiers: LCCN 2018009827 (print) | LCCN 2018015233 (ebook) | ISBN 9781502643186 (ebook) | ISBN 9781502643179 (library bound) | ISBN 9781502643155 (pbk.) | ISBN 9781502643162 (6 pack)
Subjects: LCSH: Argentina--Juvenile literature.
Classification: LCC F2808.2 (ebook) | LCC F2808.2 .M38 2019 (print) | DDC 982--dc23
LC record available at https://lccn.loc.gov/2018009827

Editorial Director: David McNamara
Editor: Lauren Miller
Copy Editor: Nathan Heidelberger
Associate Art Director: Alan Sliwinski
Designer: Christina Shults
Production Coordinator: Karol Szymczuk
Photo Research: J8 Media

The photographs in this book are used by permission and through the courtesy of:
Photo credits: Cover CDI Argentina/flickr/CC BY SA 2.0; p. 5 Thomas Müller/www.rotweiss.tv/Moment/Getty Images; p. 6 Peter Hermes Furian/Shutterstock.com; p. 7 Gabor Kovacs Photography/Shutterstock.com; p. 8 DEA/G. Dagli Orti/Getty Images; p. 9 Bettmann/Getty Images; p. 10 Eduardo Rivero/Shutterstock.com; p. 11 Chad Ehlers/Alamy Stock Photo; p. 12 Rocharibeiro/Shutterstock.com; p. 13 Buena Ventura Mariano/iStockphoto.com; p. 14 Jess Fernandez/Photographer's Choice/Getty Images; p. 15 Nicholas Smythe/Science Source; p. 16 Robert Fried/Alamy Stock Photo; p. 18 Michael S. Lewis/National Geographic/Getty Images; p. 20 Guy Christian/Hemis/Alamy Stock Photo; p. 21 Roberto Fiadone/Wikimedia Commons/File:Mezquita Centro Cultural Islámico Rey Fahd Buenos Aires 01.JPG/CC BY SA 4.0; p. 22 EyesWideOpen/Getty Images; p. 24 Awakening/Getty Images; p. 26 Marcelo Endelli/Latin Content WO/Getty Images; p. 27 Javier Soriano/AFP/Getty Images; p. 28 Wolfgang Kaehler/LightRocket/Getty Images; p. 29 Alexandr Vorobev/Shutterstock.com.

Printed in the United States of America

Contents

Introduction

Argentina is a country in South America. It is the second-largest country on that continent, after Brazil. Argentina is located between the Andes Mountains and the Atlantic Ocean.

There are many different landforms in Argentina. The country includes mountains and flat plains. There are many beautiful waterfalls and lakes. There are even glaciers in the southern part of Argentina!

More than forty-four million people live in Argentina. They are called Argentines. Some Argentines were not born in Argentina. They are called **immigrants**. Most people in Argentina live in cities.

People in Argentina enjoy many different sports and fun activities. They eat many delicious foods. They celebrate festivals and holidays with their families and friends. There is a lot to explore and love about this beautiful nation.

Monte (mountain) Fitz Roy rises over an ice field in Patagonia, a region of Argentina.

Argentina covers 1,073,518 square miles (2,780,400 square kilometers). It is surrounded by Uruguay, Brazil, Paraguay, Bolivia, and Chile. The Strait of Magellan separates a small group of islands called Tierra del Fuego from the rest of Argentina.

Argentina is located at the tip of South America.

The Andes Mountains run along the border between Argentina and Chile.

FACT!

Argentina's name means "silvery" in Spanish. Early explorers chose it because they thought there was a lot of silver in the land.

Iguazú Falls is a group of waterfalls between Argentina and Brazil. There are 275 waterfalls there.

The highest mountain is Mount Aconcagua. It is 22,831 feet (6,959 meters) tall.

The middle of Argentina has flat grasslands called the Pampas. The Pampas are dry in the east. They are wet in the south. Many cattle graze in the Pampas.

The far south of Argentina is called Patagonia. This area is very cold. Glaciers cover the land.

This is the Perito Moreno Glacier in Patagonia.

People have lived in Argentina for more than fifteen thousand years. The Guaraní were one Native group. They were farmers. Other Native groups were nomadic. That means they moved from place to place.

Ferdinand Magellan was one of the first Europeans to explore Argentina.

During the 1500s, several explorers came to Argentina from Spain. In 1536, explorer Pedro de Mendoza led two thousand settlers to Argentina. They founded the city of

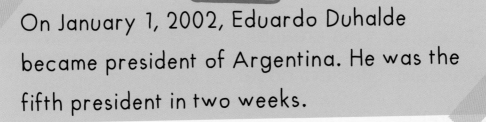
FACT!

On January 1, 2002, Eduardo Duhalde became president of Argentina. He was the fifth president in two weeks.

Buenos Aires. Spain ruled Argentina until 1816.

Former president Juan Perón and his wife, Eva.

After Argentina became independent, many immigrants moved there. However, there was fighting between different groups for power. For many years, the military ran the government. They jailed and killed many people. Finally, in 1983, the people of Argentina elected a president.

A Memorable Ruler

Juan Perón was elected president in 1946. He and his wife, Eva, became very popular. However, Perón became a **dictator**. The people and the military fought against him. In 1955, he left the country.

Today, Argentina has twenty-three provinces, or sections. Each province has a local government. The federal government makes most of the country's laws.

Presidents have lived here since the 1800s.

Argentina's federal government has three parts: executive, legislative, and judicial. The executive branch carries out the laws. The president is the head of this branch. He or she and the vice president are elected.

FACT!

Argentina's president lives in the Casa Rosada. This building is named for its pink color.

The Capital City

Buenos Aires is Argentina's capital and its largest city. Almost three million people live there.

Calle Florida in Buenos Aires is a busy road.

The legislative branch makes the laws. It has two parts, called houses. These houses are the Senate and the Chamber of Deputies. Members of these houses are elected by the people.

The judicial branch decides legal matters. The highest court is the Supreme Court. The president appoints Supreme Court judges, but the Senate has to approve them.

Argentina has seen good and bad times. During the 1920s, it was the richest country in South America. It also had a strong **economy** after World War II. But during the 1970s, the economy fell apart. Today, the economy is better.

Some of the best beef in the world comes from Argentine farms.

Cattle ranching is a big part of Argentina's economy. Argentine beef is sold all over the world. Farmers also grow wheat, lemons, peanuts, grapes, and many other crops.

There are many sheep farms in Patagonia.

Money in Your Pocket

Argentina's paper money is called the peso. Coins are called centavos. Pesos have pictures of famous people and places on them.

Argentine pesos are very colorful.

Many people also work in factories. Workers make cars, auto parts, steel, plastic goods, and leather. Argentina's mines produce lead, zinc, iron ore, gold, and copper. Patagonia produces a large amount of oil.

Many Argentines also work in the service industry, like stores, hotels, banks, and restaurants.

Argentina has many plants and animals. Large cats like jaguars and pumas live in Argentina. Monkeys live there too. Howler monkeys are the loudest. They live in the rain forest.

A jaguar in its protected home in a national park.

Crocodiles and flamingos live in some rivers and lakes. Seals and orca whales live near the glaciers in the south.

FACT!

The Pampas are too dry for large trees. The only tree there is called the ombu. Ombus can store water in their trunks.

14

Over one thousand kinds of birds live in Argentina. Parrots and toucans live in the rain forest. Penguins live on islands off the coast. Rheas run across the Pampas.

The pink fairy armadillo is an unusual, endangered animal in Argentina.

Most of Argentina's trees grow in rain forests in the north. Trees like the yatay palm trees and myrtle wood trees are protected in national parks.

Save the Animals!

Many mammals in Argentina are **endangered.** Endangered animals include jaguars, chinchillas, some types of armadillo, and several kinds of whales.

More than forty-four million people live in Argentina. Almost all Argentines are **descended** from European immigrants. Others came from surrounding countries,

Teenage girls pose for a photo during a day out in Buenos Aires.

such as Paraguay, Bolivia, and Chile. A small number are mestizos. Mestizos are people with both European and Native backgrounds. Native people make up another small group.

People have come to Argentina from other places too. These include Spain, Italy, Germany,

16

Some Argentines are descended from African slaves. Slavery was legal in Argentina until 1853.

Scotland, and Russia. Many Germans and Russians moved to Argentina after World War II to start new lives in a new country. More recently, **refugees** have come to Argentina from Syria.

Argentina's First People

Argentina's Native people make up about 2.4 percent of the population. It is hard for their culture and language to survive in the modern world.

About one-third of Argentina's population lives in or near Buenos Aires. Buenos Aires feels a lot like a city in Europe. There are tall, modern buildings. Stores and restaurants

Shoppers crowd a Sunday market in Buenos Aires.

line the roads. Cars and buses fill the busy streets.

About one-third of Argentines live along the rivers in the north. Another third lives in the south and west. Most of these areas are used for farming or ranching. People live on large ranches with lots of land for their animals.

Many poor people live in crowded neighborhoods in Argentine cities.

Argentine children go to school from March to November. They have to go to school between the ages of six and fourteen. Students study math, science, Spanish, and history. They also learn to speak, read, and write in English.

Opposite Seasons

Argentina's seasons are the opposite of those in the United States. Children have summer vacation in December, January, and February.

Religion

Most people in Argentina follow the Roman Catholic religion. Catholic holidays are important in Argentina. Argentines celebrate Christmas, Easter, and other Catholic feast days. Many towns have **patron saints**. People honor these saints

Catholics attend a service at Argentina's beautiful Salta Cathedral.

with parades. They also visit holy places to say special prayers.

FACT!

Until 1994, Argentina's president had to be Roman Catholic.

A Growing Faith

Muslims also live in Argentina. Muslims pray in mosques. Argentina's largest mosque is in Buenos Aires. It can hold two thousand people.

Some people in Argentina are not Catholics. The number of Protestants has been growing since the 1960s. Mormons are another large Christian group.

The King Fahd Islamic Cultural Center in Buenos Aires

Many Jews came to Argentina during the late 1800s. Today, about 2 percent of Argentines are Jewish. Most Jews live in Buenos Aires.

Language

Almost everyone in Argentina speaks Spanish. However, like in other Latin American countries, Argentine Spanish has its own unique words and accent.

Shoppers in Buenos Aires buy fresh fruits and vegetables from markets like this one.

Many people in Argentina also speak other languages. These languages include Italian, German, and French. Many Argentines speak

"Jaguar" is the traditional Guaraní name for a type of large, spotted cat.

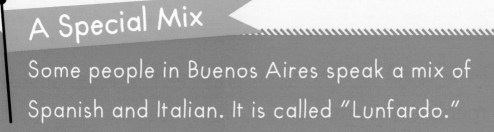

English too. Children learn to speak English in schools. Some businesses use English as well.

Traditional Native languages are still spoken today. People in the northwest speak Quechua. This language was spoken by the ancient Inca Empire in Peru. Guaraní is spoken in the northeast. The Native people in southern Argentina speak Mapuche. Mapuche is also spoken by Native people in Chile.

The biggest holiday in Argentina is Carnaval. Carnaval is held the day before Ash Wednesday. For Catholics, Ash Wednesday is the beginning of the holy season of Lent. People

Crowds admire colorful floats during Carnaval.

celebrate Carnaval by going to big parades. Marchers wear colorful costumes. There are giant **floats**. Bands play music and people dance. Carnaval is one big party!

Music and dancing are very popular in Argentina. One famous Argentine dance is the

The bandonion is an instrument found in Argentina. It is similar to an accordion. It is commonly used in tango music.

tango. Argentines enjoy many different kinds of music. Tango music and folk music are popular. So are classical music, rock, and pop.

Many Argentines love to read. Famous Argentine authors include Jorge Luis Borges and Manuel Puig.

Beautiful Building, Beautiful Music

The Colón Opera House is a wonderful place to hear an opera or see a ballet. It took eighteen years to build!

Sports are very popular in Argentina. Many Argentines play football, or soccer. Lots of people cheer for Argentina's team during the World Cup. Other team sports like basketball, field hockey, and rugby are popular too.

Lionel Messi (*right*) playing soccer during a World Cup match against Peru

Argentina's national sport is called *pato. Pato* players ride horses. While they ride, they try to

FACT!

Argentine Diego Maradona is considered one of the greatest soccer players of all time. He led Argentina to victory in the 1986 World Cup.

throw a ball into the other team's goal. Horseback riding is another common sport.

Argentina has many beautiful beaches. Swimming and diving are popular. Argentines also enjoy skiing in the Andes Mountains and in Patagonia. People come from all over the world to ski in Argentina.

Argentine Nicol Gastaldi competing at the 2018 Winter Olympmics

Olympic Gold

Argentina has won more than seventy medals in the Olympics. Twenty-one of them have been gold. Top sports include soccer, basketball, and boxing.

Food

Argentina has many delicious foods. Beef is a favorite food. People enjoy a barbecued beef called asado. They also eat a stew called *carbonada*. It includes meat, potatoes, sweet potatoes, and corn on the cob.

Tango dancers entertain a crowded restaurant.

  Empanadas, or meat pies, are also popular. People often bring empanadas on picnics. It's tasty to dip empanadas in chimichurri, which is a

FACT!

Argentines eat dinner after nine o'clock in the evening.

Drink Up!

Maté is a popular drink in Argentina. It is made from a plant called yerba maté.

sauce made of oil, vinegar, and spices.

Italian food is very popular in Argentina. People enjoy pizza, pasta, and other Italian dishes.

Maté is a favorite drink for many Argentines.

Argentines also like sweets. Cakes are often topped with a sweet caramel called *dulce de leche*. Another favorite is *alfajor*. An *alfajor* is a cookie sandwich with chocolate in the middle that is then dipped in melted chocolate.

Glossary

descended   Related to someone who lived long ago.

dictator   A ruler who has complete control.

economy   The use of money and goods in a country.

endangered   In danger of dying out.

floats   Decorated platforms that are displayed during a parade.

immigrants   People who came to a new land to live.

patron saints   Religious figures who protect a person or a place.

refugees   People who are forced to leave a country because of war or disaster.

Find Out More

Books

Morganelli, Adrianna. *Cultural Traditions in Argentina*.
New York: Crabtree Publishing Company, 2016.

Wiseman, Blaine. *Argentina*. New York: AV2 by
Weigl, 2016.

Website

Argentina Facts!

https://www.natgeokids.com/uk/discover/geography/
countries/argentina-facts/#!/register

Video

Learn About Argentina for Elementary-Age Kids

https://www.youtube.com/watch?v=FPmcmdetG54

This video includes fun facts and photos about
Argentina's geography, history, and more.

Index

About the Author

Joanne Mattern is the author of more than 250 books for children. She specializes in writing nonfiction and has explored many different places in her writing. Her favorite topics include history, travel, sports, biography, and animals. Mattern lives in New York State with her husband, four children, and several pets.